Dive in!

This book will help students, especially children, to engage with their language learning, through a playful approach of storytelling and creativity.

Peter Penguin practiced patiently

Penguin

The models also function as visual-spatial puzzles, fun exercises for creative minds to play with and gain inspiration from.

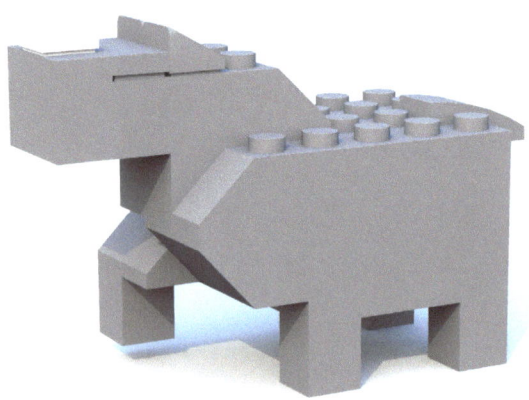

ADD to ABC
First Edition

Copyright 2019 by the Play Institute

First published in Jan 2019 by Play Institute.

ISBN: 978-87-971156-0-2

A PLAYFUL START TO LEARNING THE
ENGLISH LANGUAGE

LEFT BRAIN

Analytic thought

Language

Reading & Writing

Logic & Reasoning

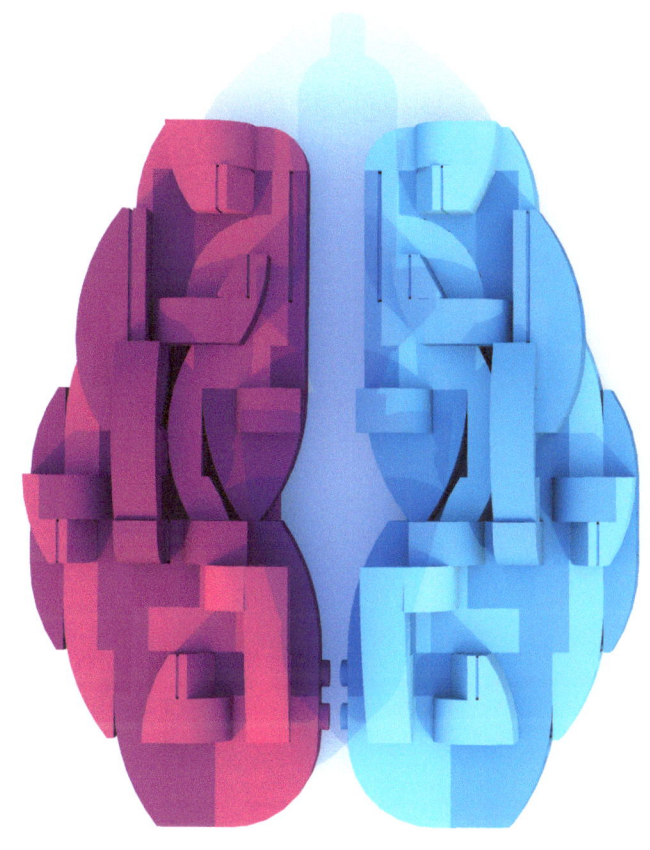

RIGHT BRAIN

Art awareness

3D forms

Creativity & Imagination

Intuition & Insight

By engaging and appealing to both sides of the brain
we aim to make the learning process become a more fun,
immersive and memorable experience for the reader.

Play.institute

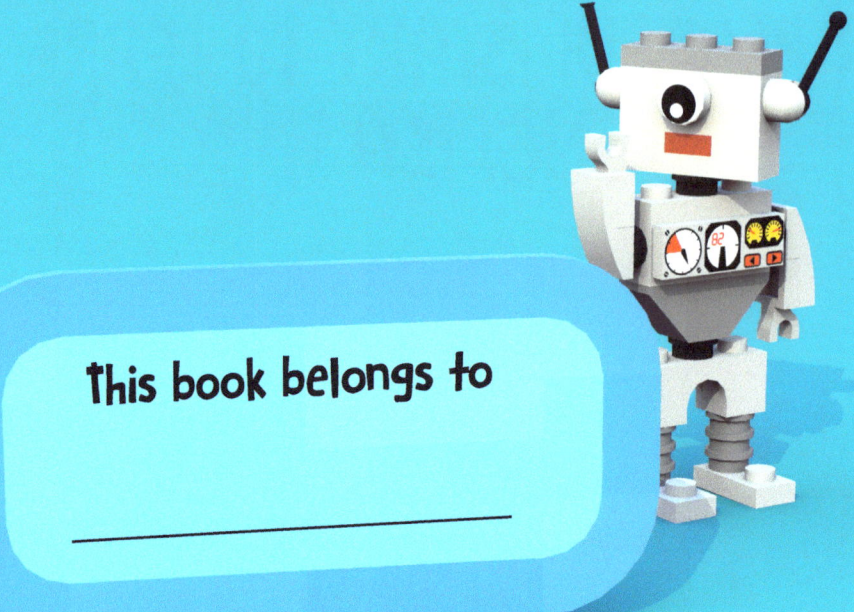

this book belongs to

_____

ADD to ABC

Designed, written and illustrated at the Play Institute

Apple

Andy always ate an afternoon apple.

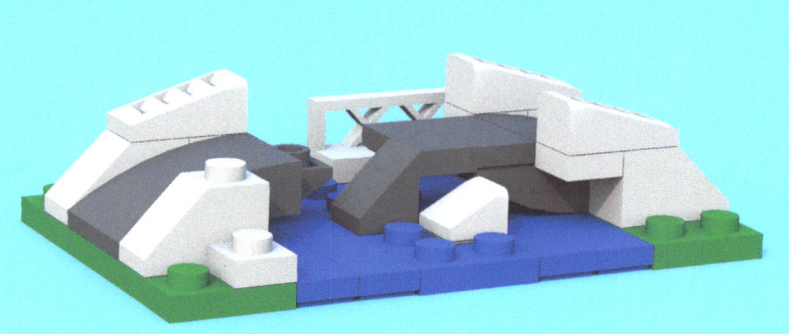

Big Bob's boat broke Bay Bridge.

Bridge

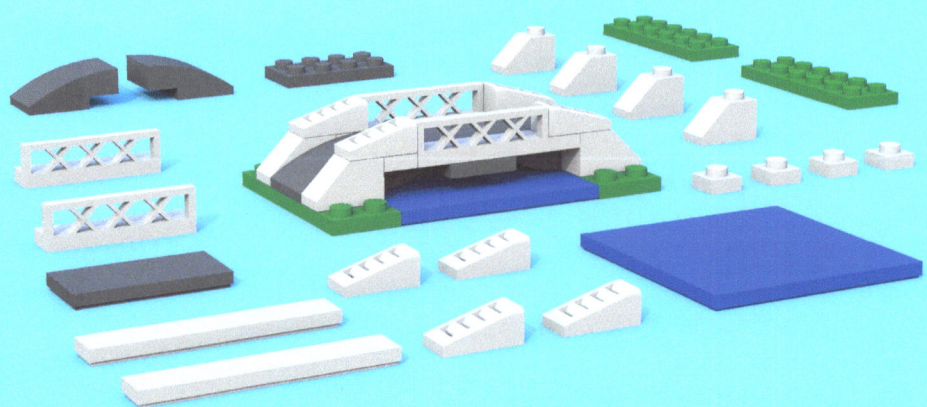

Car

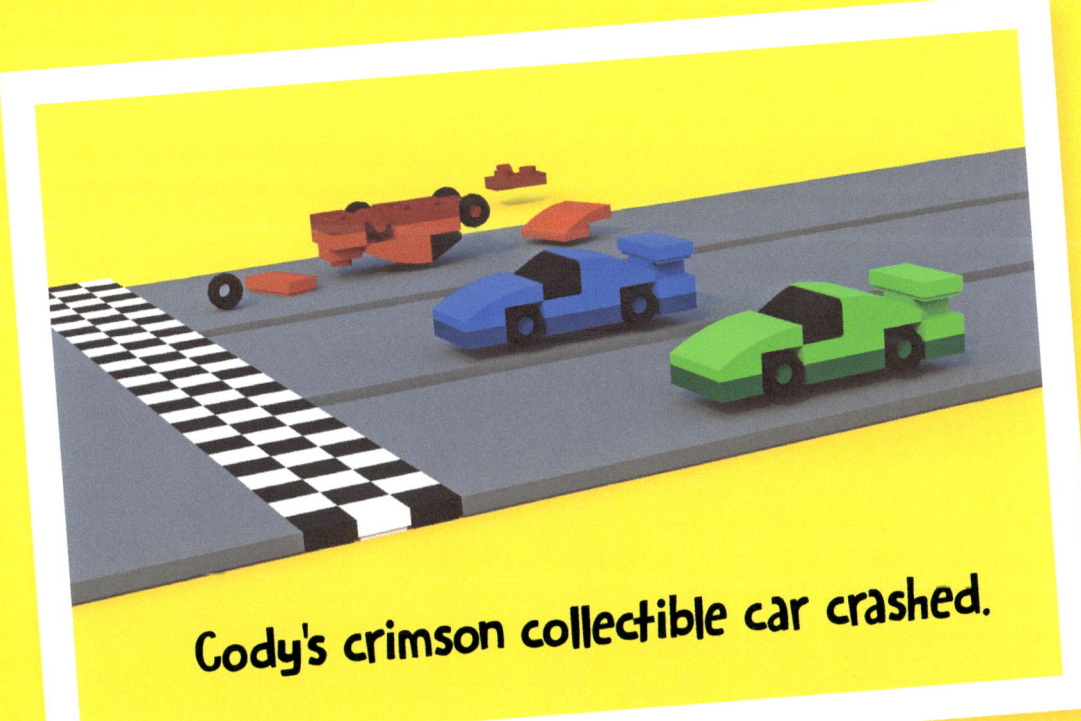

Cody's crimson collectible car crashed.

Daddy duck Dennis didn't do diving.

Duck

Eddy elephant examined every egg.

Elephant

Fox

Farm fences frustrated Freddy fox.

Giraffe

Gary giraffe generated genius gadgets.

Half Henry's house
had horrible heating.

House

Igloo

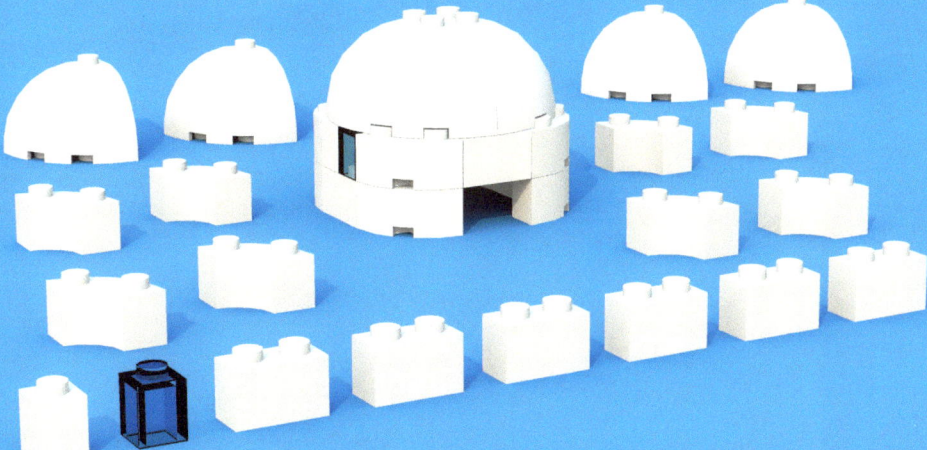

Ian's icy invention instantly increased in importance.

Jonny's jet-powered jeep jumped joyfully.

Jeep

Key

Kind knight Karen kept kingly keys.

Loyal Larry lovingly left lights lit late.

Lighthouse

Magic

Magic Max made many mouthwatering marvels.

Now, ninja Nigel never needed knives.

Ninja

Owl

Oliver owl only owned odd oranges.

Peter penguin prepared patiently.

Penguin

Quail

Quirky Quentin quested quietly.

Ron's rabbit regularly ruined remotes.

Robot

Ship

Sam's ship shoots
scary super-sized sharks.

touching taylor's treasure
triggered terrible traps.

Treasure

Unicorn

Using ugly underpants
upset Ursula unicorn.

Very venomous vipers
vexed Vinny's voyage.

Viking

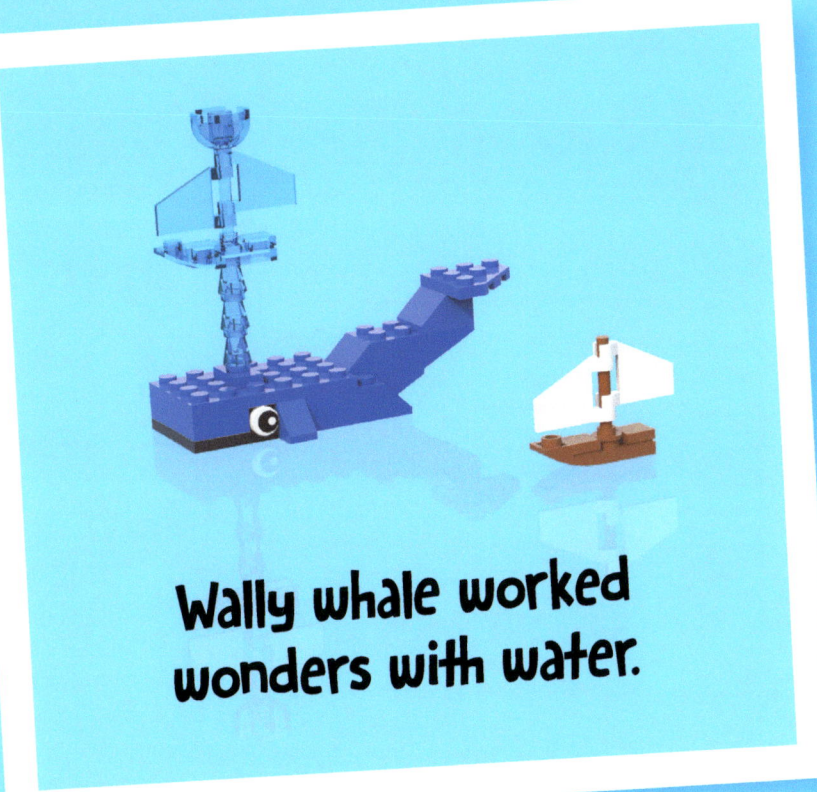

Wally whale worked
wonders with water.

Whale

Xylophone

Xavier expertly x-rayed xylophones.

Yacht

"Yummy yellow yacht!"
yelled Yoris.

Zippy Zoe, zapped
zany zombie zebras.

Zebra

CAPITAL LETTERS

A B C D E F G
H I J K L M N
O P Q R S T U
V W X Y Z

lower case letters

a b c d e f g
h i j k l m n
o p q r s t u
v w x y z

Play.institute

The Play institute aims to find the playful path to develop new products, experiences, education, insights, methods and practices.

Take the time to find,
a way to play everyday.

Lightning Source UK Ltd.
Milton Keynes UK
UKHW051004080319
338692UK00001B/1/P